THE RACING PIT
Part I-How It All Began

BY

TAOMI RAY

©December 2013

Gadsden, Alabama

One cold winter day a stray pit bull looking for a place to stay got caught by a dogcatcher and she couldn't get away.

The pup howled and barked but soon she was thrown in a cage and marked.

"Oh what now" she thought, "how can I get out of this mess I have to get out of here somehow?"

Days turned to weeks and families came
and left with short and brief meet and
greets.

No one came to her aid and she was
beginning to let her hopes for being
adopted fade until one day a deal was
made.

A family came in and paid, they actually
paid for her. She knew now she would have
it made. Yep made in the shade. No more
running the streets for her, no more being
dismayed, no more feeling lonely, alone and
afraid.

Now she gets to meet them, she gets to jump high and be happy to greet them. She wonders who they are and what they are called she just does what they say and into the back seat she crawled.

The Kingston's that's the name they had
They are a family of four two kids a mom
and a dad.

Pretty cool folks, I hope nobody is mean
and I hope nobody smokes
"I hate smoke, it makes me want to choke
but as long as they love me I guess I won't
croak".

James is the dad.
It looks like he works at some kind of
factory or at least that's what kind of bag
he had.

Florence is the mom and she is a teacher that travels around town.

She is a nice lady she gives me beef ground
round.

James Jr. is a kid.
But he tries to yell at me like he is big.

Thessaly is my favorite she is just 3.
and all she knows how to do is smile at
me☺

They even gave me a name.
Every time they call me it's the same name.
They said my name is "Queen Lady"
Kingston and that's who I became.

The Kingston's took me to a park one
afternoon to walk and play,
Boy does it feel good to have a family and
not be a stray !

But something is wrong they see a sign
that says so.
The sign said Pit Bulls can't be here so they
decide to go but Lady said "no!!"

She continued to bark and bark
because she did not see why she could not
play in the park.

"Who are these people who say I can't be
seen?"
"Who are these people that think pit bulls
are so mean?"

Back in the car they all go,
then they hear news on the radio.

A football player was in deep trouble with the law.
He was forcing pits to fight for pay. I had to drop my bottom jaw.

Queen Lady wondered, "why do people treat us this way?
 Maybe things will get better for dogs someday."

Then Thessaly spoke up and had a lot to say.
"Why was the man mean and why did he treat the dogs that way?"

Mom and dad just looked at each other and did not know what to say.

James Jr. got into the conversation by suggesting a short vacation.

"Can we go see the racing dogs run lean and strong?"
"Can we cheer for them in the crowd can we sing them a song?"

"I read about the great greyhound
and the article said greyhound racing
could soon no longer be around."

Then James Jr. looked down and frowned.

"I can see why dogs don't need to fight I
don't think that's right.
Some of these rules are too tight.
But why cant dogs race?
Isn't that after all just a chase?"

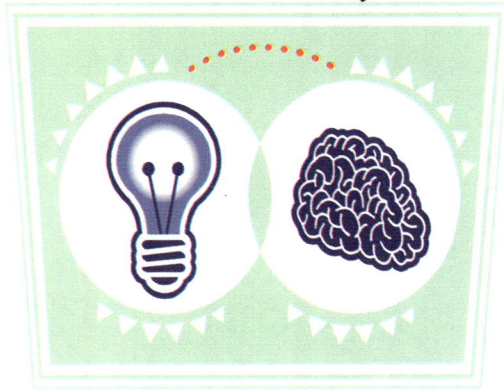

The Kingston's get home and have a lot to talk about.
They would eat at their dinner table and strategize, no doubt.

At the table James Jr. began again
"Cant other dogs run to win?"

"Why don't other dogs race, what's the
problem what's the case?"

Mom and dad just stared at each other with
frustrated looks on their face.

© Jeff Schultz/ IditarodPhotos.com

Then mom said,

"I think Siberian huskies use to race,
They are good dogs and one time they
saved a lot of people and time they didn't
waste."

Thessaly said,
"See all dogs aren't mean, they don't have
to fight, those good dogs saved someone's
life"

"Can we see the dog races, can we get
popcorn and candy?
Can we root for my favorite dog slick quick
Annie?"

"We will be real good just like the last time
you took us
"We won't argue in the car and we won't
make a fuss".

"We won't even ask for extra stuff and in that you can trust".

So mom and dad did unanimously agree.
Their family went to see the greyhounds
and were happy as can be.

When the family came back they talked
about building their own racetrack.
A homegrown racetrack.
And they would build it with their hands
from scratch.
I don't think I have ever seen anybody do
that.

Soon I would be bred.
Like the ritzy call "thoroughbred".

My puppies were going to race in a lane.
My puppies would be racing to change their
name.
My puppies may even bring fortune and
fame.

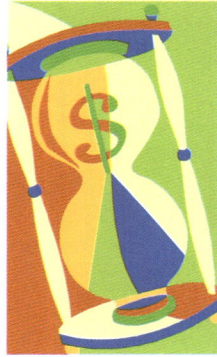

The next day the Kingston's went on
errands together in town.
They came back with goods new and they
spread cheer around.
They were so happy I wanted them to tell
us what they found.

They went to the hardware store to buy

tons of tools.
Lawn equipment and things they could use.

They drew up plans to clear two acres of
land the mom inherited from her uncle in
Georgia.
The dad also had a small piece of land from
his prosperous relatives in Florida.

The project would begin with building a

brand new shed.
The family would have to build it to be the place where all my puppies would have a bed.

Then they would build a racetrack.
A quiet little field with dogs racing in the back.
People could donate one dollar to get in.
They could buy popcorn balls and candy and cheer for their favorite dog or pup to win!
It is all about to begin.
They did it all just like they said!

They built a shed and a racetrack in the back and I was bred.

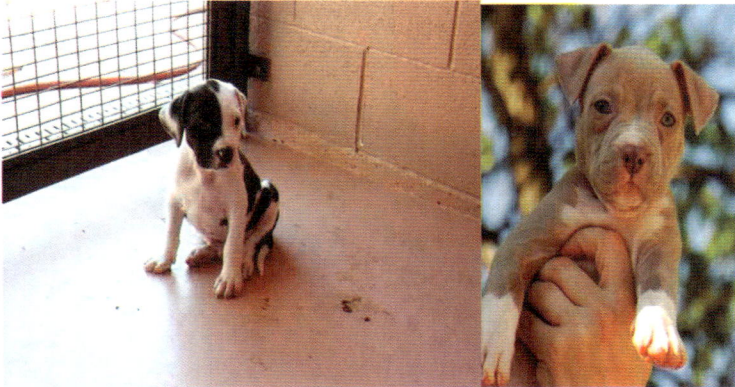

My first puppies came and they all got a great name.
Janie's Got a Gun and *March Rain* are going to bring fortune to the dog world, we will have dog fame!

I wonder will they only race other pit bulls or will they have to run against a Great Dane.

For now I will just keep worrying about each individual name.

Seven puppies are the first of the pride. Stay tuned for the rest of the story it's going to be a great ride!

THE END

To Learn more about "*Breed Specific*" legislation, see the link below:
http://www.buzzfeed.com/chelseamarshall/37-pictures-that-will-restore-your-faith-in-pit-bulls

https://petitions.whitehouse.gov/response/breed-specific-legislation-bad-idea